This is How I Fight My Battles Workbook

Copyright 2019 by Patricia Simon

THIS IS HOW I FIGHT MY BATTLES WORKBOOK: MY FIGHT CLUB WITHIN
Copyright © 2019 by Patricia Simon

All Rights Reserved. This book may not be reproduced in whole or in part, in any form or by any means, mechanically or electrically, including photocopying, recording, or by any information storage, printing, retrieval known systems or future invented without prior written permission by the author.

This book is my memoir. It is simply about my step-by-step journey to how I have learned to accept, and take care of, my full self. It is how I choose to live my life and how it works for me. This book is for entertainment only, and neither the author nor the publisher can guarantee your success nor provide medical advice. Also, the information in this book, cannot supplant professional advice from a physician or other doctor. If you feel you need emotional or medical support, please seek the proper medical personnel.

Project and Line Editor: Patricia Simon
Contributing Editor: Liz
Cover Design: Dominic
Illustrator: Elena R. Brown

Library of Congress Cataloging-in-Publication Data

Simon, Patricia.

This is How I Fight My Battles Workbook: My Fight Club Within/Patricia Simon

p. cm.

ISBN: 978-0-578-77178-6

1. Self-help   2. Memoir

In Praise of *My Fight Club Within*

"Patricia, thanks for your inspirational writings and being 'real.' Your awareness is key and spot on! The truth is hard to swallow sometimes but sharing with others is healing! It has been such a blessing to call you a friend. Best wishes on your continued journey we call life!" **~Regina E.**

"Dear Patricia, *My Fight Club Within* was so relatable. The honesty and transparency in your story are truly authentic. I could feel your vulnerability turn to strength as the words on every page formed a perfect picture in my mind as if I went on this journey with you. I'm excited to see where life brings you. My new friend, you are unstoppable! Sincerely with appreciation." **~Trish B.**

"*My Fight Club Within* is an eye-opening read that really equips you with the tools to fight your battles to first love yourself and then be able to love others. This is a great guide to leading your life and other lives to personal freedom!" **~Patrick O.**

"*My Fight Club Within* is a very realistic book with struggles that everyone deals with. In this book, you will find the realism of life and the different options to take to live it to the fullest. It's up to you to actually implement these words of wisdom in your life and truly live in complete freedom." **~Dawson E.**

"*My Fight Club Within* is soulfully written and embraces life's experiences with such relatable experiences. Patricia's ability to come to self-realization of her past, turning it into an amazing journey, brought to light some of my personal inner controversies as well. I applaud her bravery and look forward to my personal journey to come." ~**Brooke W.**

"Patricia Simon's metaphor of the boxing ring is inspired. Through her examples and struggles we can all gain strength to follow our own paths and gain confidence." ~**Christine H.G.**

"*My Fight Club Within* was inspiring as I am on my own personal journey to self-love and acceptance. Let your inner spirit guide you through, and you shall prevail." ~**Charlotte H.**

"A splashy poolside tell-all blended perfectly with the hard-earned lessons of a seasoned and thriving survivor; Patricia Ann will win your heart and make you a better person in the process. A wild ride, a warm hug, an honest and crystal-clear view through the eyes of a true-hearted beauty. Just try to put it down!" ~**Elizabeth A.**

"What a privilege to be given the rare opportunity to see our world through the eyes of someone like Patricia Simon. With her vividly captured thoughts and unique writing style, she is gifted with the ability to virtually paint the pictures of her mind inside your head. I believe she has miraculously turned a challenge into a triumph with her book, *My Fight Club Within*." ~**Mark G.**

TABLE OF CONTENTS

Introduction i
1. Spiritual Warfare..1
2. Soul Awakening 4
   My Wake-up Call...5
   MFCW Book Cover Description 6
3. How I Fight My Battles..8
   Love, Joy, and Peace 9
   Red, Yellow, and Green..14
   Awareness, Action, and Allow 19
   Patience, Kindness, and Goodness 21
   Black, White, and Gray 27
   Faithfulness, Gentleness, and Self-Control 30
   Forgiveness, Myself, and Others 40
4. The Fruits of the Spirit 47
5. Fighting Your Battles 55
   Round 1: Fear 55
   Round 2: Sadness 58
   Round 3: Anger 61
   Round 4: Happiness..64
   Round 5: Surprise 67
   Round 6: Disgust 70
6. My EAT PRAY LOVE 74
   Eat...74
   Pray (SPIRIT)...77
   Love 81
Epilogue..85

Introduction

Welcome to my book, *This is How I Fight My Battles Workbook*, which is meant as a companion to my book, *My Fight Club Within* (Figure 1). If you haven't purchased or read the book, I highly recommend that you do. By doing so, you will obtain the most benefit from these exercises. The book is available on Amazon, Barnes & Noble, IngramSpark, and other online resources. This workbook is a companion to the book and is not a standalone book.

Figure 1: *My Fight Club Within* Book

My hope in sharing *This is How I Fight My Battles Workbook* is that together we may experience growth in a deeper sense, realizing that we are so much more than what we see as a reflection of ourselves on the outside. In fact, our image is so different from the very same image of ourselves that others see. We are such beautiful and unique, one-of-a-kind beings with an awesomely divine spirit that beams with a power that can only be driven with your permission. Your spirit will never input force on you against your will. Spirit can only proceed by your total surrender in love.

When I speak of my unique CHILD within, I speak of my unique child within as a vestige reminder of my early years. I full-heartedly believe that through sharing my experiences from history to present, I will demonstrate many challenges I face daily, especially with having a learning disability that my dad couldn't accept and forced me to keep hidden.

This sweet child of mine may merely be acting out in ways that she never had the chance to actually experience, reveling in the opportunity to feel her own feelings now. I recall quite clearly the example of sadness. It's a Sunday evening, and my mom is dropping off a much younger version of me after a long, fun day. Little Patty goes inside with teary eyes, already missing mom. Daddy says flatly, "Stop your crying; you'll see her again next Sunday."

Many similar instances over the years have ingrained deeply in me a path for running away from my inner child, which is timeless in me. This path leads to peaceful light out, radiating pure love and joy. I was told to avoid sadness and cover up my tears.

In corner two, ADULT ego awaits its turn to push in and take over as boss, pointing its finger exclaiming, "I know what's going to happen here next. Mark my words as I can clearly see what the outcome will be!"

As an ADULT, when led by my SPIRIT, I exude patience, kindness, and goodness.

The BODY, flesh, which contains my faithful heart, gentle soul and feet that ground me into the earth, when they are walking in self-control; not-so-patiently waiting in corner three, comes out swinging, swallowing its convulsions to be dealt with later.

In corner four, stands the light of SPIRIT. The SPIRIT is my guiding light that leads and directs only when I am present. SPIRIT is

LIGHT that instantly drowns out the darkness and turns my bad and ugly into goodness. The SPIRIT peacefully waits for the opportunity to radiate its effortless power of resolve, not to overcome the others, but to uplift and embrace the fullness of each member of the fight.

Yep, that's me in my personal war-zone battleground with and within myself. My CHILD is continually complaining about her same old silly past ouchies. My ADULT ego is ablaze with concern, worried solely with self-preservation. My BODY is all wound up in a tizzy, hyperventilating into a paper bag. As my true SPIRIT awaits my cry to relinquish my all.

How do I get to my safe place out of the ring and out of being stuck and alone in those dark corners? How can I assist my SPIRIT with moving from the oppressed and tiny, smoky amber hue to beaming out in full radiance?

My SPIRIT will only lead me when I relinquish my control. It is only in the present moment when I let go (of my ADULT ego, my CHILD and BODY) that I become equally yoked with my total being. I must get out of my ego head, release worries about the past or future, and be in the present moment so my SPIRIT can lead me. My heart is connected, and at one with the entire universe. In that present moment, my tiny spark ignites into a flame of purity and clarity. I step out to be my true self, in love, joy, peace, patience, kindness, goodness, faithfulness, gentleness, and self-control.

Only when I finally extended my inner self out to the universe, am I able to receive, embrace, and engage, experiencing that oh-so-wonderfully fabulous moment of true oneness. Residing within that alignment, I can recognize all the love that is, and has always been, right there within my reach.

My transformation began taking form with these three simple steps:

Step 1. Awareness – if I feel

Step 2. Action – I can heal

Step 3. Allow – and be real

PATRICIA SIMON

"Be confident and true to yourself."

1. Spiritual Warfare

On the front cover of *My Fight Club Within* is a photograph that was taken many years ago of a sunset somewhere in the Midwest (see also Figure 2 if you don't have the cover). I don't know who took it or even how it got into my hands. However, it has become one of my most prized possessions that hangs up high on my wall.

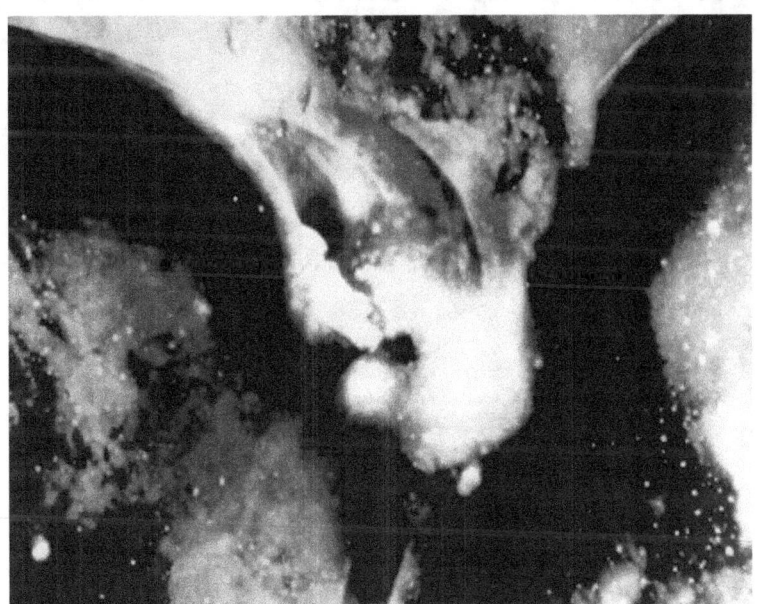

Figure 2: *My Fight Club Within* **Front Cover Photograph**

On the right half of the picture, I see an Angel. After displaying the photo for over ten years hanging on my wall, my son Patrick came into my room one day, and said, "Mom, that's a creepy and ugly demon staring into the face of the angel."

"What! Where?" I said. "I don't see it!"

It was at that very moment when I finally saw it. There it was just as clear as day – it's pointy ears and beady eyes staring up at my beautiful angel. Patrick and I immediately in unison uttered, "Wow, this is spiritual warfare."

Oh, how freaky and weird that was for me. Talk about the heebie-jeebies! I took the picture down and put it in the closet and tried to forget about it. To have something before your eyes and not see the obvious. After all, my thoughts were "Hell no" in my Alabama accent at the time as this east coast girl was trying to fit in as a southern belle in my showcase home. No way will I have that ugly demon with my beautiful angel displayed on my wall. I was torn.

This is my shortest chapter because there is no better way to explain it then by sight of my book cover of *My Fight Club Within*; for you to see it directly through the eyes of the beholder.

This is how I fight my battles.

THIS IS HOW I FIGHT MY BATTLES WORKBOOK

"Keep your feet grounded being SPIRIT-led."

2. Soul Awakening

It was soon after the discovery of the demon in my Spiritual Warfare picture, towards the end of January 2009, and I was still married, and my husband was working out of town; all my kids were away at school. I was alone in the big empty house with my four-legged best friend, Cookie. At 5:00 a.m., I awoke to an astounding voice that echoed out, "Patricia Ann, it is time for you to wake up now. Patricia Ann, it is time for you to wake up now."

I was shaken and chilled to my bones as I arose and leaped out of bed, shouting out, "Who are you? Who is there?"

I immediately grabbed the phone and the alarm clock asking again, "Who is this, who is here? Please, please answer!" No response. There was no one there.

Later that day, my son, Patrick, had come home, and I shared with him what had happened. I was still shaken to my very core by that voice, like no other, and how it repeated twice and called out my name. It was clearly the most brilliant, masculine yet feminine, and perfect tone of authority, an alive sounding vibration to my ears that immediately woke me from a deep morning sleep.

Patrick then shared with me a CD by Jason Upton that he wanted me to hear. I listened while he played it on the computer. He asked that I pay close attention and listen to hear if that was like what I had heard earlier in that same likeness of voice. I listened; goosebumps rose and took hold of my entire body as I listened in awe. "Yes, Oh my God!"

Then he shared the story of Jason Upton, a soloist who was performing somewhere in the Midwest before a live audience. Shortly after his performance, a twelve-year-old boy came up to the artist and said how he enjoyed his band.

Jason said, "There is no band. It was just me by myself." The boy proceeded to say, "Oh no, there was you and all your choir, dressed in white singing in the background with you." Please, go ahead, *Google* it.

My Wake-up Call

Since that very day, I believe, wholeheartedly, that it was God who woke me up and told me, "Patricia Ann, it is time for you to wake up now. Patricia Ann, it is time for you to wake up now."

So, I began to face my demons by proudly displaying once again one of my most prized possessions of art. Not only back up on my wall, but now I want to share it with the entire world; my photo of the demon and the angel that is now on the front cover of this book. Now you have the full story of my picture of Spiritual Warfare captured up in the sky for you and me.

Be aware that you may not see the angel and demon at first. In fact, there are some friends that still have not been able to see. Please be kind and patient with yourself and don't allow my beliefs, your beliefs, or un-beliefs to have space for room of any judgment.

MFCW Book Cover Description

My best way to describe this picture for you is that the angel takes up the entire middle and right side all in white and rose and outlined in light gold. The height and width of the angel take up far more space than the demon, starting at the very top of the pure white wing. It's majestically large, with deep tones of gold color crown on top of its head, which is in front of the white wing. Under the crown, tumbles thick, curly, golden hair, outlining the side profile of the face and around the left ear. The angel's detailed side profile is directly gazing over its own white rounded shoulder blade with the wing adjacent upward toward the top. You can see an all-white face from the side, with the forehead deeply darker in gold tone, drawing down to the humble dark golden left brow with the perfect white nose, lips, and chin outlined lightly. You'll see just a small, almost circular shape of black sky in between the chin, wing, and round shoulder and only the top part of the white neck and chest. Remember that all the angel is white with gold lining throughout. Surrounding the angel on the very top center and top right you'll notice rays of lavender and rose, unlike the familiar color scale. The picture has many orbs of different shades of rose, white, gold, and pink.

The demon is much smaller with its bald, coned head on the very left side of the picture. It appears to be looking out into the black sky not even seeing the angel dominating over it. There is only a tad bit of a dot of white on the right side of the demon's big, ugly, deformed nose with no brightness or shadows of light. The entire demon is a mere smudge of a smeared dark reddish black on the lower left-hand side of the picture. What I noticed most prominently when I became aware of the creature is its pointed ears and specks for its beady black eyes.

I feel there is never a time that I must wait for my angel to appear for my angel is with me at all times. I am convinced wholeheartedly that on January 25, 2015, when my mom died, not only just my angel but also my mom's angel was there together in connection in love for us.

Angels are omni.

This is how I fight my battles.

This workbook goes hand-in-hand with *My Fight Club Within*.

3. How I Fight My Battles

First comes love, then comes marriage. Yes, I took the big step, but with myself. In fact, my wedding reception is still present now within me. I committed to love, honor, and take care of myself till death do I part.

I, _____ (your name), commit to love, honor and take care of myself till death do I part.

The first nine chapters in *My Fight Club Within* and this workbook were inspired from these scriptures of Galatians 5:22-23 (KJV), "But the fruit of the Spirit is love, joy, peace, longsuffering, gentleness, goodness, faith, meekness, temperance: against such there is no law."

Throughout this workbook, you will be asked to fill in answers. The more honest you are with yourself, the more growth you will experience. Your responses are for you only, so don't be shy. If you can't be honest with yourself, then who?

"You yourself, as much as anybody in the entire universe, deserve your love and affection." ~Buddha

"Never leave a true relation for a few faults... Nobody is perfect. Nobody is correct at the end. Affection is always greater than perfection."
~Buddha

"No one saves us but ourselves. No one can and no one may. We ourselves must walk the path."
~Buddha

Love, Joy, and Peace

Love. They say it's what makes the world go around, the common denominator between us that connects and ties us all together in this cosmic universe. It's also noted that it's impossible to love another if you don't love yourself first.

Hate is a place where I will admit to having dwelled much too often. Even amidst such chaos, I had no clue at the time that I was in a prison of my own making. I was embroiled in, and far too preoccupied with, operating from the wounds of my past. At the time, this was what I knew, and it felt like my comfort/safe zone.

Leaning into my transformation, I decided to honor this significant change with a deeply personal ritual. First comes love, then comes marriage. Yes, I took the big step, but with myself. In fact, my wedding reception is still present now within me. I committed to love, honor, and take care of myself till death do I part. This is my never-ending love story, my soul-written vows from within. There is no beginning and no end.

There is only now.

> *"If I love myself, I love you. If I love you, I love myself." ~Rumi*

Sorrow rolls into shock and awakens my inner being with a gut-jerk reaction inside my knotted throat as my belly begins to ache. Again, the seats are taken in each corner of the boxing ring within my being. Dark clouds were now blanketing over those beautiful rays of sunshine while the soft waves are now crashing thunder within.

My SPIRIT is timeless. However, when my all-time-consuming ADULT ego, fearful CHILD, and turbulent BODY react to bad news, look out! The sh*t is about to hit the fan.

Here I go into the next round of suffering. Damn, it hurts, and it hurts badly. I choose to face it and not run away. I remember that everybody suffers, and millions are suffering as well at this very moment. I'm not alone, and I am only human. I am going to switch on my light, group hug, cry if I must, maybe get on my knees on the side of my bed, and beat my pillows for five minutes. I will deal and fully feel this sorrow of heartbreak. However, I will not stay here; I will allow these emotions to be as the clouds that are constantly shifting. I choose to shift with them and not to remain stuck.

Joy leaps out as I'm practicing yoga at the beach on a beautiful sunshiny day in January 2019, breathing in the fresh, salty air as the waves splash up on the sand.

My mind is totally in alignment with my heart when breathing into every cell of my body. I am grinning from ear to ear in total bliss with my spirit dancing. Leading from within, I feel complete and one with the other people as we are dancing on clouds after a beautiful class. Suddenly, my cell phone buzzes, and I answer with a happy "Hello?" Much to my surprise, I received devastating news that I tested positive for tuberculosis. News like this will test your will of spirits, and fortunately for me, it was a false reading.

When confronted with stressful situations, be sure to remember the joy in your life.

"It is in the nature of things that joy arises in a person free from remorse." ~Buddha

List the things in your life that bring you joy.

_____

_____

_____

_____

_____

Peace readily arrives and is present in those joyful moments of being in love. In loving myself first, I can love you and others. On my daily walks, in any venue, as long as there's nature, trees, or water, is where and when I experience peacefulness; in those magnificent moments of full presence. I can be alone, with my lover, a friend, or even a pet.

I have found that my personal peace from within is what is most important for me. I do cherish my newly found peacefulness in every single breath I take.

My commitment to keeping my peace is to remain calm and exercise my breathing throughout the day.

Sometimes at night, I'll wake up as if in a panic with a choppy and shallow breath. I'll then slowly begin reciting a prayer, focusing on breathing slowly in and out on each word, allowing my soul to be nourished and flourish. It usually works as I tend to peacefully go back to sleep with my SPIRIT gently caressing my nighttime existence.

During the day, in practicing my breathing, I may have to exert more effort and energy when the choppy, shallow breath sneaks in. My CHILD loves swimming against the current while my ADULT intellect demands that my BODY/belly continue the practice of exercising deep and full breaths in and out. It is when I stop all the things that I feel must be done with great immediacy and do nothing except breathe, my happy SPIRIT veils over me with its crown of glorious peace.

Anxiety can come over me without warning, the very moment I start worrying and thinking about my future or dwelling on my past. Fear can set in quickly, stealing my peace with worries such as, "Will I have enough money? Why didn't I tell him how I was feeling?"

Grrr... here comes that telltale clearing of the throat and then down to my unsettled tummy. All the while, my SPIRIT is yearning for a group hug and the opportunity to illuminate the way out of this silly nonsense.

I will go back into my peaceful state of walking in love and light; for it is impossible to feel anxiety when I am fully present. I will be thankful and live in this moment, experiencing peace and joy within. I then plant a big, big smile on my face and at the same time, try to frown to test myself.

Frowning impossible, I have succeeded.

"Those who are free of resentful thoughts surely find peace." ~Buddha

"Peace comes from within. Do not seek it without." ~Buddha

How may you find love in your life?

_____

_____

_____

_____

How may you find joy in your life?

_____

_____

_____

_____

How may you find peace in your life?

_____

_____

_____

_____

Red, Yellow, and Green

RED. I Stopped to obey my SPIRIT. By surrendering my all, I was then able to be aware of the LIGHT that shined in the place (Castle) and person (Liz). My heart had to be totally open (even if my mind was closed) to allow all the amazing new things and people to develop in connecting as one with my being.

"Stop, stop. Do not speak. The ultimate truth is not even to think." ~Buddha

Slowing down for YELLOW, I am giving my SPIRIT opportunity to lead in favor of my BODY resting fully present in its own unique and natural rhythms. I am healing while my mind (ADULT ego) is clear and present in actively becoming reacquainted with its brilliant and precious CHILD who is happy and now able to play freely.

Going GREEN after the abrupt stop on RED before YELLOW is all necessary for allowing my now authentic self to be me.

I craved for true intimacy with myself. Through seeking help with, and from, my friends, teachers, and therapist, I realized I had to do the demanding work myself. I would not experience instant gratification. I had to invest before I would get a return.

There would be no person, no place or thing that would distract me and hold me back.

I would no longer peg my happiness on external things such as in other people, places, and things as I am ultimately always going to be disappointed. That's why it is so important to find the happiness that exists inside of me. No one can take, alter, or change that.

> *"Every person you meet will perceive who you are at that moment. When you bring the past with you, they are seeing you as all the things you drag in. Try to leave the day behind and embrace the moment you're in so they see you for who you truly are."* ~Trish B.

I listened and then acted to face up to my dysfunctional poor behavioral patterns.

To name a few of my poor behavioral patterns: running away, catastrophizing, and constant disappointment.

Name three of your own poor behavioral patterns:

1. _____

2. _____

3. _____

Now it is your turn for your SPIRIT as you begin your commitment to your true self. If you have read *My Fight Club Within*, you understand the concept of how I fight my battles. How will you fight yours?

_____
_____
_____
_____
_____
_____
_____
_____
_____
_____
_____
_____

When will you stop at the RED?

_____
_____
_____
_____

Name some ways you will slow down for the YELLOW.

___

How will you go full throttle to GREEN?

___

Amazingly beautiful results are beginning to spring out on your GREEN pastures from your RED stop and slowing down for YELLOW. Describe your moments.

___

When you are disappointed, what do you do?

___

How can you structure your life to deal with disappointments?

_____

_____

_____

_____

What joy do you have in your life that when you are disappointed you can always reflect upon?

_____

_____

_____

_____

Awareness, Action, and Allow

My transformation began taking form with these three simple steps:

Step 1. Awareness – if I feel

I stopped my running after slowing down my rapid pace, fueled by my constant disappointment in myself and others.

Step 2. Action – I can heal

Suffering stops for me the moment I let go of my mind's ego and control by trying to fix myself and others.

Step 3. Allow – and be real

By surrendering all my disappointments with forgiveness first in me and then in others, my true and radiate favor shines brightly out and unleashes miracle upon miracle.

List the three "A" steps to transformation.

Step 1. _____

Step 2. _____

Step 3. _____

Step 1. Awareness – if I feel.

What negative emotions are you feeling?

_____
_____
_____
_____
_____
_____
_____

What hurt are you currently experiencing?

_____
_____
_____
_____
_____
_____
_____

Step 2. Action – I can heal.

What steps can you take to start the healing process?

_____

_____

_____

_____

_____

_____

Step 3. Allow – and be real.

What do you have in your life that you need to be honest about to yourself?

_____

_____

_____

_____

_____

_____

Patience, Kindness, and Goodness

Patience, first with myself, is imperative as I feel this is my weakest area that I must face daily. I feel the heavy desire to have all my needs met promptly and addressed ASAP.

I have just taken up meditation and find that practicing first thing to begin my day makes a huge difference. Patience is a practice that must be honored moment by moment, led by my SPIRIT. It is especially important to cultivate and remain focused on deep breathing. My regular flow (or mantra) is "Let breath in... let breath go. Let Go!"

Mantras are important as they become a guiding force in your life. It is critical that you develop a mantra and memorize it.

What mantra do you have in your life?

_____

_____

_____

_____

_____

Write your mantra on sticky notes or index cards and post them around your house as a daily reminder of how great you are.

Share your mantra with your family and friends and explain to them why it is important to you.

Is there a second mantra you can develop? Write it here.

_____

_____

_____

_____

_____

"Endurance is one of the most difficult disciplines, but it is to the one who endures that the final victory comes." ~Buddha

"If you propose to speak, always ask yourself, is it true, is it necessary, is it kind?" ~Buddha

Kindness is a daily practice and gift that I begin with the first thing each day. As soon as my eyes open every morning, I rise with tender loving care to me first.

Being kind to myself within enables me to walk in the purest form of connection that I extend genuinely and lovingly throughout my day to others.

Yes, when I walk in the presence of love, joy, peace, and patience, kindness is then ingrained as a significant attribute that others see instantly in me. Especially with children, just one look is all it takes and its automatic love. Babies and children sense and know that they're safe with me. My gift and the most passionate job I do and have is working with children. Being present in the company of children enables my soul to be fresh, ready, and young. Together, our spirits play as one.

"Have courage and be kind. For where there is kindness there is goodness, and where there is goodness there is magic." ~Cinderella

Patience and kindness and goodness, oh my! It's so plentiful for me and you; why? Because it's free, and it's everywhere. It's good to be alive. I so look forward to waking up each day, being grateful that I can rise while watching out my window as the sun peeks up over the water.

I may then spend some time meditating, maybe take a walk on the beach or a bike ride and purposefully go out of my way to smile while giving eye contact and greeting others, saying good morning to as many peeps as I can.

I love spending time with being kind to myself and having plenty of goodness that is genuinely and gracefully coming out of me and ricocheting amongst others.

What are you grateful for today?

_____

_____

_____

_____

_____

Repeat this positive affirmation:

"I can do the possible because I have already experienced the impossible. I can do what I make up my mind to do."

However, I also realize that I must understand that I'm not going to feel good all the time. After all, I remember, I'm only human.

What things tend to get you down in the dumps?

_____

_____

_____

_____

_____

Make up your mind that you are in control of your happiness and no one else.

Black, White, and Gray

I absolutely love and adore all three of these colors, as my wardrobe and home decor are mostly black, white, and gray. However, when I was growing up with my strict dad, he often would use the phrase, "It's either BLACK or WHITE, right or wrong. Now speak up and answer me with the truth." You know what's funny? As I think back on this, ninety-nine percent of the time I would always tell the truth, and my dad would never punish me for my honesty. My mom, on the other hand, would love to say, "Make sure you get our story straight with your dad in this little white lie, okay, Patsy?"

Never would I agree and lie for my mom.

So that's when I discovered the color GRAY. The silence was my gray in not speaking at all on the matter with a simple nod of a poker face in silence or in giving no reply at all. Until one day, my mom and I were out shopping, and she had me pull over for lunch getting a hearty cheeseburger to satisfy our appetite. She was adamant for me not to tell her husband that we had lunch. She knew better than to ask me to lie as early on in my broaching adulthood I had my healthy boundaries intact with my parents.

We walk into my house with full bellies from our massive burgers and fries; my mom runs in to use the bathroom. Then her husband appears and asks me, "Have you eaten?" I could not hide my truth. He could tell by the grin on my face that I had eaten, and then he asked, "What did you have?"

I replied, "A burger."

Then, all at once, my husband comes in the backdoor at the same time my mom walks into the room, and he announces he is starving, "how bout I cook some burgers on the grill?"

Mom's husband repeats, "Yes, honey, how would you like to have a juicy grilled hamburger?"

Mom goes onto say, "Yes, I can't remember the last time I had a good hamburger."

Steve, her husband, was so pissed at her and called her out on her boldfaced lie. She was pissed at me for not keeping her WHITE lie a secret.

I'm cracking up all over again in just writing this true story down. I miss mom.

Heaven, Hell, Purgatory...

I will admit that by living in the GRAY area, and keeping my secrets, the truth is hidden in my silence. It is like Purgatory, in the middle of nowhere.

Is BLACK a bottomless hole on top of WHITE and what the f*ck does color have to do with anything?

So, who out there believes there is a Heaven, Hell, and Purgatory, and who doesn't? Also, why does it matter? It doesn't matter. What matters is when you find yourself stuck in a world of staying awake all night wrestling with your problems and losing sleep over them.

In wanting change, you must do the demanding work, you simply have to dig deep down within to some dark areas that you have been avoiding like the plague.

Okay, this section is not to be absorbed with thoughts about the past, future, life, or any thinking in which we tend to get lost. This adds absolutely nothing to our true self. We must lose ourselves to find ourselves. We must let go of all the silly nonsense that really doesn't matter.

My story of black, white, and gray was something that I felt the need to share. It is interesting that I associated these three colors to try to make sense out of nonsense. Your turn now. How do you feel about what I just wrote?

In your own words, apply Black, White and Gray to yourself?

What are the white areas of your life?

What are the gray areas of your life?

_____

_____

_____

_____

_____

What are the black areas of your life?

_____

_____

_____

_____

_____

Faithfulness, Gentleness, and Self-Control

Faithfulness is being true to myself as I remind myself daily of that beautiful commitment and vow, I made to myself. Faithfulness always goes hand-in-hand with accountability. I hold myself accountable by investing in myself.

I get therapy and seek out assistance when I feel stuck inside a boxing round too long.

It's a beautiful gift to be faithful, accountable and true-to-self by receiving help when I need it. Outstanding results can then occur, getting me back on track, resulting in again walking in faith with love to myself and others. I committed to myself in the first chapter of this book, and I'm holding true and keeping my vows.

"Faithful is Being Steadfast in Affection or Allegiance; Loyal" ~ from Merriam Webster Dictionary

What is faithfulness to you?

___

What things in your life are you accountable for?

___

Do you have an issue with accepting help from others? Why or why not?

___

When was the last time you asked for help from someone? Describe your circumstances?

_____

_____

_____

_____

_____

How did you benefit from the help you received?

_____

_____

_____

_____

_____

Gentleness with me is key. Being an empath gives me a significant advantage in connecting with others because I have that built-in soul connection. I know and realize the importance of gentleness with myself firsthand as my energy is continually wanting to explode within. My gentle, loving spirit must be in control, leading me, because when I'm experiencing other people, their own issues quite easily take over.

> *"However many holy words you read, however many you speak, what good will they do you if you do not act on upon them?" ~Buddha*

What is gentleness to you?

___

Going back to your gray, black and white areas of your life, reflect on the three.

White Area:

What white area lessons have you learned?

___

Gray Area:

What gray area lessons have you learned?

___

Black Area:

What black area lessons have you learned?

_____
_____
_____
_____

If you could tell your younger self one thing, what would it be?

_____
_____
_____
_____
_____
_____
_____
_____
_____
_____
_____

"Never to suffer would never to have been blessed."
~Edgar Allan Poe

Self-Control is keeping my commitment to love. In being true to my commitment, my inner soul radiates out into every move I make. Daily my emotional intelligence grows and matures, but I must always check in with myself first, "What's going on with me? And, what do I need to do?"

Facing my truth first is what sets me free, allowing my Spirit to lead the way.

What is self-control to you?

Do you have an issue with self-control? Why or why not?

When was the last time you felt out of control? What happened?

What lesson or lessons did you learn from the outcome?

_____
_____
_____
_____
_____

What do you wish you would have done differently?

_____
_____
_____
_____
_____

How do you identify when you are getting out of control?

_____
_____
_____
_____
_____

Who in your life can you count on as your support backup?

_____

_____

_____

_____

_____

Why is this person important to have in your life?

_____

_____

_____

_____

What other support systems do you have in place?

_____

_____

_____

_____

_____

_____

Forgiveness, Myself, and Others

    I have an exotic and unique look about me with having light eyes, dark hair, and olive skin. I'm often misconstrued for a lot of different nationalities, especially when I'm visiting other countries as I tend to blend in.

When I first was married and visiting Mexico, the border officials separated me from my husband and retained me at the Tijuana border in a small room for questioning for over an hour. My adrenaline was pumping still out-of-control from just going parasailing for the first time; so, nothing could top that in frightening me.

The questioning centered around those touchy subjects that some people struggle with to have an intelligent conversation, and instead, would rather attack with their truth and how they feel you should believe. Then it turns into a fight if you should disagree or voice your opinion on the subject matter.

All wars throughout history have involved the beliefs and egos of powerful people, such as kings and queens, and their need to rule, dictate, or otherwise impose their beliefs on others. Playing God is a tough role. Nobody is perfect, qualified, or equipped for His job.

> *"It is better to conquer yourself than to win a thousand battles. Then the victory is yours. It cannot be taken from you, not by angels or by demons, heaven, or hell." ~Buddha*

I grew up with f*cked-up stuff such as politics, religion, Black and White shoved down my throat by my dad and a passive mom who had no boundaries or morals she cared to speak of. But I respected, accepted, and loved my parents just as they were.

My mother would never tell me she loved me until I taught her how. Her mother died when she was two, and she grew up in an orphanage. What does her dad go out and do soon after his wife dies? He marries a younger woman and has three more baby girls to add to his seven kids that he gave away. He then decides he'll keep the new wife and kids.

I miss my mom every day, and my dad; hmmm, maybe once a week. They were amazing parents doing the best they knew how, and for that I am grateful. I learned from their mistakes, witnessing the years that were wasted in the dark on their stubbornness, unforgiveness, judgment, bitterness, guilt, and self-hatred.

My dad, for example, was a brilliantly intelligent and handsome man who sacrificed his life in his prime years in raising me. He obeyed the Catholic Church in never remarrying. Big mistake, because I feel my dad would most likely still be alive, had he followed his heart in love. So, I could have maybe had a cool stepmother to add to my village of love.

When you give, give, and give and never receive back all the love that's out there in the universe, you lose yourself.

My mom was a thorn in my side for many years as I never could understand her abandoning me at the age of five. The pain was so incredible in my early adulthood years because my mom was downright jealous of me. I didn't talk to her for two years when my kids were babies.

I had bought my mom a plane ticket to watch my kids while my husband and I took a five-day vacation in Mexico. After returning home from my trip, my neighbor down the street, who I barely knew, came into my home with a ten-page nasty letter about me that my mom had written to her. Kate, my neighbor, said, "I don't even want you to read this, but your mom said terrible, awful things about you, and I know for a fact they are not true. I feel bad that I played a part and listened to her gossip about you, (her only daughter) here in your beautiful home."

Science says we need four essential elements to survive – water, food, air, and light. Water is always running over like a stream in our SPIRIT when we are active with our BODY taking the guided steps that breathe in and out the flow of air we do not see. Food nourishes our BODY just as our breath allows life that we count on for survival.

SPIRIT is the Light of the world creating all, including us, into existence.

I am grateful, again, for my parents in giving me life, taking care of me, and for our healthy and loving relationships that we formed during their later years.

Love without judgment.

> *"To understand everything is to forgive everything."*
> *~Buddha*

> *"Forgive those who insult you, attack you or take you for granted. But more than this, forgive yourself for allowing them to hurt you." ~Buddha*

Now let's get down to the hard work. Your responsibility is to be YOU. How do you feel about your relationship now with your parents (even if they are absent or deceased)?

_____
_____
_____
_____
_____
_____
_____
_____
_____

For what things have you forgiven them?

_____
_____
_____
_____
_____
_____
_____
_____

For what things have you forgiven yourself?

_____
_____
_____
_____
_____
_____
_____
_____

Have you let go of all the hurt, anger, worry and guilt by not blaming them and yourself? If not, what are the things for which you still find yourself complaining, criticizing, and judging?

_____

_____

_____

_____

_____

_____

_____

_____

_____

Who or what are your thorns?

_____

_____

_____

_____

_____

_____

_____

_____

_____

Will you release it now? Yes, let's agree it is time to let go of that childhood rooted fear. We are now adults, and we agree not to let those scary memories ruin our beautiful lives. Feeling the pain and releasing it to your SPIRIT will free you instantly.

What is your action plan to release your thorn or deep childhood fear?

_____
_____
_____
_____
_____
_____
_____
_____
_____
_____
_____
_____
_____

4. The Fruits of the Spirit

We are all unique human beings, and our pains and suffering are on all sorts of levels. Keeping them buried is where we get stuck in a rut that ruins any chance of experiencing a real, mature, authentic, happy, and loving relationship that we so deserve. Instead, blurred vision causes us to only go through the motions in a brain fog mode.

My Foundational Steps for Change are:

1. **Love** – You must first love yourself. Doing so will bring about the healthy results you're wanting.

What changes do you need to make to love yourself to achieve the healthy results you desire?

_____
_____
_____
_____

2. **Joy** – Spending time with others, walking, laughing, and smiling is key. Having a generous heart is how you will experience a joyful spirit.

   What actions can your take to spend time with others so that you can experience a joyful spirit?

   _____

   _____

   _____

   _____

   _____

3. **Peace** – Being alone in nature looking at the trees, water, and animals will wrap you in perfect peace.

   Where can you go to spend time alone in nature?

   _____

   _____

   _____

   _____

   When was the last time you spent time alone in nature?

   _____

   _____

   _____

   _____

What benefit did you receive from spending time alone in nature?

_____

_____

_____

_____

Set a date to spend time alone in nature. How will you remember to adhere to it?

_____

4. **Patience** – Deep breathing, journaling, and smiling a lot are some of the ways to practice patience with yourself and others.

   Identify areas in your life that you need to develop more patience with yourself and others.

_____

_____

_____

_____

What actions can you take to develop patience with yourself and others?

_____

_____

_____

_____

Identify your triggers that identify that you are losing your patience with yourself or others.

_____
_____
_____
_____
_____

5. **Kindness** – Show kindness to yourself and others. This creates a healthy environment within you and around you.

Look at your surroundings. How can you show kindness to yourself and to others, right now?

_____
_____
_____
_____
_____

When was the last time someone showed you a random act of kindness and how did that make you feel?

_____
_____
_____
_____
_____

Identify three people in your life that could benefit from a random act of kindness from you.

1. _____

2. _____

3. _____

Make plans to deliver a random act of kindness to the three people you identified above. Then, execute your three random acts of kindness plans.

Plan 1

_____
_____
_____
_____

Plan 2

_____
_____
_____
_____

Plan 3

_____
_____
_____
_____

6. **Goodness** – Be good to yourself and others. Doing so brings goodness back to you. This, too, creates a healthy and nurturing environment for you and others.

How do you take care of yourself?

_____

_____

_____

_____

7. **Faithfulness** – Believe in yourself and believe that you will focus on and move forward with the good things you are accomplishing. Have faith in what your heart is telling you to be, to do, and to have.

On a scale of 10, being the highest, and 1 being the lowest, what is your faith level?

_____

What can you do to either maintain your faith level, or increase the level? Be specific.

_____

_____

_____

_____

_____

_____

8. **Gentleness** – Gentleness with yourself is key, for it is the only way you can give gentleness to others.

   How are you gentle with yourself?

   _____
   _____
   _____
   _____
   _____

   In what ways can you improve on your gentleness?

   _____
   _____
   _____
   _____

9. **Self-control** – Setting appropriate boundaries in your life turns overindulgence and excess into healthy choices that help produce the life changes that you want.

   Reflect on your life. Where do you need to set boundaries?

   _____
   _____
   _____
   _____

Define your action plan to set boundaries in your life.

_____
_____
_____
_____
_____
_____
_____
_____
_____
_____
_____
_____
_____

"Chaos is inherent in all compounded things. Strive on with diligence." ~Buddha

5. Fighting Your Battles

Imagine inside, within our core, a black boxing ring. There are four corners. There inside sits an immature CHILD in corner one, and an ADULT ego in corner two, jittery, tensed-up BODY in corner three, and charged-up SPIRIT in corner four. Your SPIRIT-light patiently waits to unleash the endless power of true freedom.

In each of the six rounds that follow, you will recall a different life example of a battle where your ADULT ego, BODY, CHILD, and SPIRIT were all interacting within a fight. Each round is centered around a different human emotional situation. You will describe what was going on with each of the four parts of you, and then provide the outcome of the battle. We are starting with Round 1. Here we go!

Round 1: Fear

My life battle example of a Fear situation would be in October 2018, when I went from traveling the world with my six-foot-three Aussie boyfriend, with him holding my hand every step of the way, to being by myself, getting a sweet little one-bedroom place in paradise, surrounded by views of the water. I'd gotten out of a relationship, moved to a new city and knew absolutely no one. I was alone and on my own for the first time in my life. I didn't like it one bit.

What is your life battle example of a Fear situation?

_____
_____
_____
_____
_____
_____
_____
_____

What part was your ADULT ego playing in the fight?

_____
_____
_____
_____
_____
_____
_____
_____

What part was your BODY playing in the fight?

What part was your CHILD playing in the fight?

What part was your SPIRIT playing in the fight?

___

What was the battle outcome of this Fear situation?

___

Round 2: Sadness

My life battle example of a Sadness situation would be when I was working things out as I wrote my book. I was adapting to the beach life. I was learning to chill. Even if I was a crybaby, I was in cleansing with my tears, and nothing was holding me back. It was my wedding party, and I would cry if I wanted to.

What is your life battle example of a Sadness situation?

___

What part was your ADULT ego playing in the fight?

___

What part was your BODY playing in the fight?

What part was your CHILD playing in the fight?

What part was your SPIRIT playing in the fight?

_____
_____
_____
_____
_____
_____
_____
_____
_____

What was the battle outcome of this Sadness situation?

_____
_____
_____

Round 3: Anger

My life battle example of an Anger situation would be when I think of one of my favorite quotes from my cousin, Gail. I'd been experiencing a difficult time in my life, and the choices that led me there had been my own. "Patsy, have you eaten enough turds yet?" I was so pissed off at myself and others for taking all their crap out on me, or even for taking my own crap for that matter!

What is your life battle example of an Anger situation?

_____
_____
_____
_____
_____
_____
_____
_____

What part was your ADULT ego playing in the fight?

_____
_____
_____
_____
_____
_____
_____
_____

What part was your BODY playing in the fight?

_____
_____
_____
_____
_____
_____
_____
_____

What part was your CHILD playing in the fight?

_____
_____
_____
_____
_____
_____
_____
_____

What part was your SPIRIT playing in the fight?

_____
_____
_____
_____
_____
_____
_____
_____

What was the battle outcome of this Anger situation?

_____
_____
_____

Round 4: Happiness

My life battle example of a Happiness situation would be when I discovered the Tiki Bar at my new place in paradise. I'd squeeze myself in amongst all the happy couples that were there either vacationing, honeymooning or on a fun work-related trip. I was envious as I observed how perfectly love fit snuggled in between all these beautiful people. I would make conversation. But, just beneath the surface of this conversation, my real feelings arose.

What is your life battle example of a Happiness situation?

___

What part was your ADULT ego playing in the fight?

___

What part was your BODY playing in the fight?

_____
_____
_____
_____
_____
_____
_____
_____
_____

What part was your CHILD playing in the fight?

_____
_____
_____
_____
_____
_____
_____
_____
_____

What part was your SPIRIT playing in the fight?

_____
_____
_____
_____
_____
_____
_____
_____

What was the battle outcome of this Happiness situation?

_____
_____
_____

Round 5: Surprise

My life battle example of a Surprise situation would be when I was chosen to participate in a song and dance performance in Italy. The performer came over to my table, singing out to me while gently taking my hand and bringing me out on the floor. We danced a full tango, my first tango, complete with an extravagant dip. Then much to my surprise a roar of applause and a standing ovation. I felt brave, with my kind loving and gentle spirit, which allowed me to go up on stage and trust in a singer and dancer.

What is your life battle example of a Surprise situation?

___

What part was your ADULT ego playing in the fight?

___

What part was your BODY playing in the fight?

_____
_____
_____
_____
_____
_____
_____
_____
_____

What part was your CHILD playing in the fight?

_____
_____
_____
_____
_____
_____
_____
_____
_____

What part was your SPIRIT playing in the fight?

_____
_____
_____
_____
_____
_____
_____
_____

What was the battle outcome of this Surprise situation?

_____
_____
_____

Round 6: Disgust

My life battle example of a Disgust situation would be when I was sixteen and had just found out that my friend had been being raped by her dad. My heart was utterly broken that day for my friend. It made perfect sense as to why she was like she was. There would be no apology accepted or allowed by my friend on behalf of her dad to me. Never would I expect my friend to be sorry or apologize to me for the evil acts of her dad. Nor did I want her to experience any guilt for leaving me alone with that monster.

What is your life battle example of a Disgust situation?

_____
_____
_____
_____
_____
_____
_____
_____
_____

What part was your ADULT ego playing in the fight?

_____
_____
_____
_____
_____
_____
_____
_____
_____

What part was your BODY playing in the fight?

_____
_____
_____
_____
_____
_____
_____
_____

What part was your CHILD playing in the fight?

_____
_____
_____
_____
_____
_____
_____
_____

What part was your SPIRIT playing in the fight?

_____
_____
_____
_____
_____
_____
_____
_____
_____

What was the battle outcome of this Disgust situation?

_____
_____
_____

6. My EAT PRAY LOVE

Lots of challenging work has gone into developing healthy habits that are done every day now for me as I am committed to taking fantastic care of me.

One of my most important healthy habits is forgiveness to myself. Be aware that it is imperative that I practice this daily. I also give myself permission to act with compassion the moment I abandon myself with thoughts of unworthiness.

> *"To keep the body in good health is a duty... otherwise we shall not be able to keep our mind strong and clear."* ~Buddha

Eat

Another very important healthy habit is eating. Or at least it can be healthy. What is available to be eaten today is much different than it was 100 years ago. It is so important that we make informed food choices. It is also important that we are actively doing things that are good for us, and that we have guidelines for protecting us against things that are not good for us.

Below is my personal list of foods that I eat, which work for me. I always buy organic.

1. Fish
2. Egg Whites
3. Green Beans
4. Broccoli
5. Sprouts
6. Spinach
7. Kale
8. Brussels Sprouts
9. Any Type of Deep Greens (such as leafy salads)
10. Cauliflower (look up healthy recipes)
11. Blueberries
12. Blackberries
13. Raspberries
14. Strawberries
15. Almonds (raw)
16. Avocados
17. Ginger
18. Herbs (garlic, turmeric, oregano, others)
19. All Live Food (rooted and grounded organically)
20. No Processed Foods
21. No Creamy Dressings (use vinegar & olive oil)
22. Cook with Coconut or Olive Oils

What follows now is my personal list of general activities that I regularly do that work for me.

1. I eat (BODY maintenance).

2. I drink plenty of structured water.

3. I balance my energy by practicing Tai' Chi Gung.

4. I exercise by walking, dancing, and yoga.

5. I breath steady with meditation.

6. I volunteer at the Children's Hospital.

7. I brush my teeth with fluoride-free toothpaste.

8. I bath daily with coconut soap.

9. I get plenty of sunshine.

How can you incorporate the above list into your life?

_____
_____
_____
_____
_____
_____
_____
_____
_____
_____

Finally, below is my personal list of general guidelines that work for me. You may find some of them beneficial to incorporate into your life.

1. Move as much as possible (walking, hiking, biking, etc)
2. No food after 6:00pm (if you are trying to lose weight)
3. All food portions should fit in the palm of your hand
4. No white or fried foods (sugar, potatoes, rice, flour, breads, etc. or fried chicken, fried fish, fried rice, French fries, etc.)
5. No negative self-talk
6. Never drink alone; never before 6:00pm (unless on vacation)
7. Never drink more than 2 drinks in a 3-hour period (if out)
8. Use paraben-free and aluminum-free deodorant
9. Turn off Bluetooth; unplug electrical items where you sleep
10. Detox from television, internet, and mainstream news and social media (read and meditate in its place)
11. Drink plenty of water, instead of eating food, when you're hungry after 6:00pm
12. Journal every day before going to bed and you will sleep better and develop a better habit
13. Work on yourself – it takes thirty days to change a behavior

Pray (SPIRIT)

Every morning before I get out of bed, I thank the Most High and name something that I'm grateful to have in my life.

Next, as I walk into the kitchen while making my coffee, I have recent pictures of me with all my kids, and I pray over all of us for protection and guidance.

What are you grateful for in your life?

___

What is your morning ritual?

___

How can you add prayer for your family into your morning ritual?

_____
_____
_____
_____
_____
_____
_____
_____
_____

I journal, meditate and walk every day and try to remember to do one random act of kindness. I like to think of how that may change three hundred and sixty-five lives, yearly. When I can't sleep or am overthinking, I pray this Bible prayer from Matthew 6:9-13 (NKJV):

"In this manner, therefore, pray:

Our Father in heaven, Hallowed be Your name. Your Kingdom come. Your will be done on earth as it is in heaven.

Give us this day our daily bread. And forgive us our debts, as we forgive our debtors. And do not lead us into temptation, but deliver us from the evil one.

For Yours is the Kingdom and the power and the glory forever. Amen."

Research the Bible and memorize three scriptures that you can include in your morning prayer.

Scripture 1:

_____
_____
_____
_____
_____
_____
_____

Scripture 2:

_____
_____
_____
_____
_____
_____
_____
_____

Scripture 3:

_____
_____
_____
_____
_____
_____
_____
_____
_____

Love

Love is an energy, a smile, an appreciation, an outrageous force of being grateful, hopeful, and generous, with an open heart.

> *"If anything is worth doing, do it with all your heart." ~Buddha*

When I finally took that first step out from within in committing love to myself, favor made way surrounding me with endless possibilities. I found that men were more attracted to my confidence instead of my body.

While teaching classes in the Castle, members and guests clap at the end of my classes, complimenting me on my choreography and exotic moves. I found that I now love my car dealership (even better than my other that I missed) by communicating my true feelings.

They respond with excellent service resulting in me giving them a five-star rating on *Google*.

I get my hair done weekly for free at the Castle, and in exchange I am personally coaching and teaching one on one. I eat free meals at the Castle and the Children's Hospital, so I hardly ever need to buy groceries. I walk or ride my bike to work on the beach and save the wear and tear on my car. I have my favorite shops and coffee spots that I now meet all my beautiful and lovely new friends.

What favorable things happen for you when you love yourself?

_____

_____

_____

_____

_____

_____

_____

_____

> *"Maturity is learning to walk away from people and situations that threaten your peace of mind, self-respect, values, morals and self-worth." ~Buddha*

Healthy people that I now attract (MFCW) are not only work-related professionals, but they are also my go-to friends that welcome, support and embrace my ideas. We spend hours of cheerful and quality time together enjoying deeply optimistic conversations.

Honestly, when I first moved here, I had no job, no friends and was clueless as to what I was going to do next. I seriously started buying scratch-offs and researched on how to play the lottery, joking with my kids, but not really, that that was my new job.

However, looking back now at where I started and where I am at now is living proof of my SPIRIT at work in love with me. I am happy and proud of my brave self.

"Happiness will never come to those who fail to appreciate what they already have." ~Buddha

I started drafting this book, *This is How I Fight My Battles Workbook*, two years ago as a manual for services provided by me as a fitness coach in helping people to lose weight. I was so busy being busy in life in accepting my dysfunctional behavior, thinking, Oh, well, I'm okay. At least that's what I thought. I had all the forgiveness down for everyone except for me – love and forgiveness to myself. It was me not letting go of all my fear of the unknown.

Six months ago, while in a conversation with my awesome teacher, Raz from Hoffman, he advised me to stop reading all these Self-Help books and instead just read a novel. I was infected with fear and so obsessed with fixing myself. My CHILD was out of control inside, and my BODY was weeping endlessly because of a clueless ADULT ego mind that was a tank of worry in search of answers.

My deepest desire and wish for you is to be encouraged and inspired after you have read the very last word on the very last page in your workbook here. I hope that your most actual essence of all your innermost magnificent, powerful energy of radiant love bursts out in planting your sloppiest wet kiss ever on *This is How I Fight My Battles Workbook*. We will forever throughout eternity be spiritually connected as one in this universe – rooted, grounded, and founded by love in you and me.

There is no ending to our love story. For now, I take leave of you with one of my most favorite scripture verses:

> *Matthew 7:7-8 (AMPC) – "Keep on asking and it will be given you; keep on seeking and you will find; keep on knocking and the door will be opened to you. For everyone who keeps on asking receives; and he who keeps on seeking finds; and to him who keeps on knocking, the door will be opened."*

Epilogue

My fight club within (self-love) has always dwelled deep inside me. I feel we all start created in love regardless of how our parents feel or felt about each other in our hour of conception.

Every human being is unique and comes from a one-of-a-kind seed, and one-of-a-kind and unique set of seeded parents. Regardless of who they are or have become, some may be total dicks or the opposite, living like Mother Theresa. One fact that cannot be ignored and must be acknowledged is that the seed was formed, making a baby, and that baby is you.

There is a MAJOR difference in you being you and me being me.

If I dare say or write this, I became obsessed with love in maybe wanting too much, so much that my heart has been overflowing and bursting out since the moment I felt my baby girl inside me.

I smothered my kids with love and affection and still do but in a healthy measure.

Yes, from observing my parents' good qualities, those of Ms. Sue and Mr. Howard, my dad's next-door neighbors, Carl and Mary (my mom's next-door neighbors), and Lillian and Whitey, neighbors across the street from my mom, I was able to offer the many facets of pure love to my children.

So, I had three happily married couples as my surrogate parents with sixteen kids between them that were my playmates and siblings. I had more love and attention constantly pouring out onto me than my own parents, Fred and Vera, could ever dare compete with.

My dad, Fred, was the only child from his wealthy Catholic dad (also Fred) migrating from Germany with his Jewish wife, Anna.

My mom, Vera, was the youngest child of seven. Her poor dad migrated from France with her mom, who was Cherokee, Irish, and Canadian. She died at the age of twenty-eight when my mom was two.

Having four sets of parents, with all their uniquely flawed characteristics, taught me so much about the importance of valuing myself. I learned from them how to be a best friend, wife, daughter, and mother. That's how I raised my kids, enforcing all their beautiful values and good manners and respect for themselves and others.

This is a good thing that I want to highlight here in *This is How I Fight My Battles Workbook*. If anyone of you out there were to have the privilege of meeting any of my kids, you would have the pleasure of experiencing extremely intuitive, intelligent, and caring human beings.

My Fight Club Within has been a work of pure love and bliss that I had been pouring out onto others more so than onto myself.

I finally "get" it or better yet, "get" me.

My astrological sun sign is Libra, the scales. It is very important and necessary for me to have everyone and everything in its place. Balance and structure are key in getting me through my dyslexia in everything I do.

I have learned how to finally be alone with myself by fighting my ongoing battles – battles I have very much enjoyed sharing with you through words written in love and awareness expressed throughout these pages.

Facing my truth and awareness, my guilt and shame, from the secrets buried deep within, which by the way were rooted in love and understanding all along, I acted out in destructive patterns such as running away and avoiding important adult decisions which were a necessary process in stepping into real freedom. I was stuck way too often, even when I was in a healthy, loving relationship and felt my life was beautiful and in perfect balance, the truth lingered – a truth I have finally accepted.

My Fight Club Within has been the organic work of the step-by-step progress in the opening of my heart, which has produced outstanding and miraculous results as these once dry bones inside now contain and exude my ocean of love. I am still a work in progress and, as I have reiterated all through this book, we are humans, nobody is perfect, and we will continue to discover life, especially when making our very own perfect mistakes.

Writing this book in these past ten months has been my longest and hardest walk (fight). It has, however, altogether been the fight that has turned into the peaceful walk I have so needed to become me.

My journey with *My Fight Club Within* began ten years ago with my wake-up call, "Patricia Ann, it is time for you to wake up now. Patricia Ann, it is time for you to wake up now."

The hard work had begun with a lot of deep, deep soul digging, removing layer by layer the toxicity that was weighing me down. I was numb and only existing through my masked BODY and the shell of a pretend ADULT ego in Pat-world. The first step was awareness, which took place immediately upon my wake-up call. I had to take the necessary steps of going into my CHILD fantasy fairytale directly into the woods, keeping my eye on that small flicker of light (SPIRIT) for my truth and reality.

I had to go into my fairytale to come out. Yes, I jumped down into many rabbit holes in facing some of my greatest fears. I experienced more adventures that I learned to love and had deep and hidden desires for but had no idea of what I truly wanted. My hidden desires and dreams have all come alive and true, and my nightmare of loneliness has ended.

Yes, *My Fight Club Within* has a happily-ever-after ending to my fairytale-come-true. This is my true conception of endless love (SPIRIT) where my inner beauty resides in and radiates from deep within me, connecting us by that same kind of deep and true inner beauty that is rooted and grounded in you. This love is grounded within the soil, connecting our steps in this vast universe, and finding one another in the epic air we all breathe.

Traveling throughout the world in each little town, village, city, and state with my Aussie boyfriend hand-in-hand with me every step of the way, we met many extraordinarily beautiful people that would sit down with us and share their personal stories. I'd picture these people as fitting into my sixteen siblings and us dwelling in as neighbors maybe even living next door or across the street in one big, lovely community.

At the time, I couldn't conceive just how much depth, width, and height my heart could consume inside my being while living out my truest heart's desires.

As I will continue my path with my heart wide open, on my journey, being led by my SPIRIT; there is no place to escape my love. Please allow me to introduce myself. Patricia Ann.

This is how I fight my battles.

How the best brainstorming sessions end…

PATRICIA SIMON

WORKBOOK IS BASED ON THIS BOOK!

MY FIGHT CLUB WITHIN

AVAILABLE

Amazon, Barnes & Noble, IngramSpark,
and other online retailers

Get in Touch

www.patriciasimonwriter.com

NOTES

NOTES

www.ingramcontent.com/pod-product-compliance
Lightning Source LLC
Chambersburg PA
CBHW071409290426
44108CB00014B/1750